All Siblings Are
Important

Words and Artwork That Celebrate
All Sibling Relationships and
the Feelings They Bring

Written and Illustrated by Laura Camerona, CCLS

A **Words Worth Repeating** Book

This book is dedicated to my own brother, Sam. My own first expereince in loving someone who works and thinks differently than myself.

Book best suited for children ages 3-14.

ISBN 979-8-9873529-1-5 Paperback

www.wordsworthrepeating.com

I am a sibling.

Siblings are brothers or sisters. A lot of the time, it means that your parent has more than one child.

But, kids can have cousins, neighbors, or friends who are just like siblings. I might be a special kind of sibling to someone who doesn't have the same parents as me.

Families can be big with lots of siblings,

or families can be small.

When you are in a family, you are a part of something.
I am a part of something bigger than me.

I am a piece in our family puzzle.
I am an important member of our family team.

Although it might not always feel like it, one sibling is never more important than another sibling.

All siblings are important.
No matter the age. No matter the size.

You may have just become a sibling for the first time,
or you may have been a sibling your whole life.

But, once you are a
sibling, you are a
sibling forever.

Why are siblings important?
Do you wonder?

Siblings make you stronger.

Siblings make you faster.

Siblings make
you kinder.

Siblings make
you laugh.

Siblings make
you cry.

Siblings help you learn important things.

Siblings help you learn some not-so-important things!

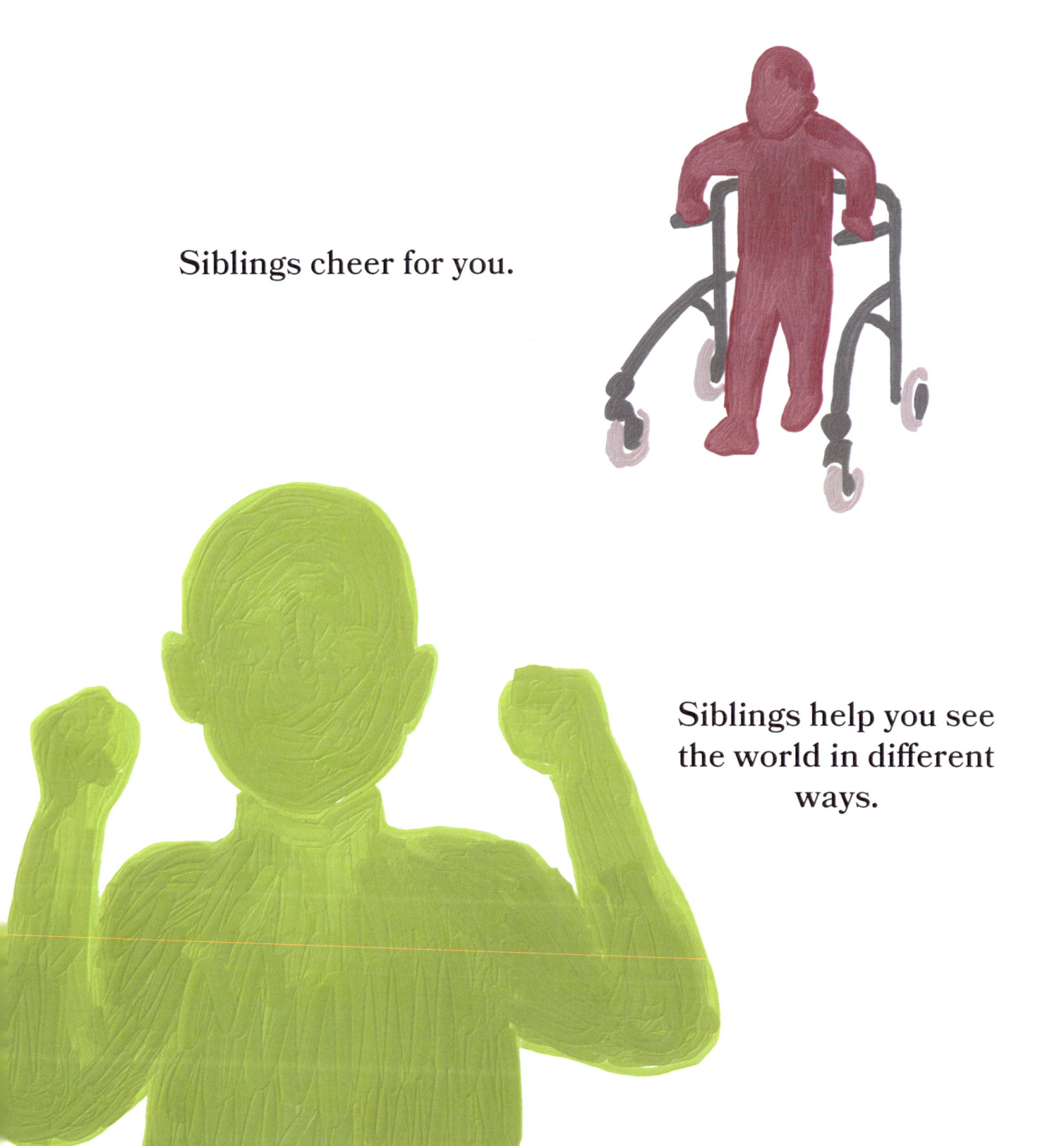

Siblings cheer for you.

Siblings help you see the world in different ways.

Siblings help you with
hard things.

Siblings know when you don't need help
and can do it on your own.

Siblings make some days more fun.

Siblings make some days more frustrating.

Siblings understand
each other, in ways no
one else can.

Some days, siblings don't
'get' each other.

Siblings can have
the best time when
they are together.

Siblings can also
drive each other nuts.

Siblings miss each other
when they are apart.

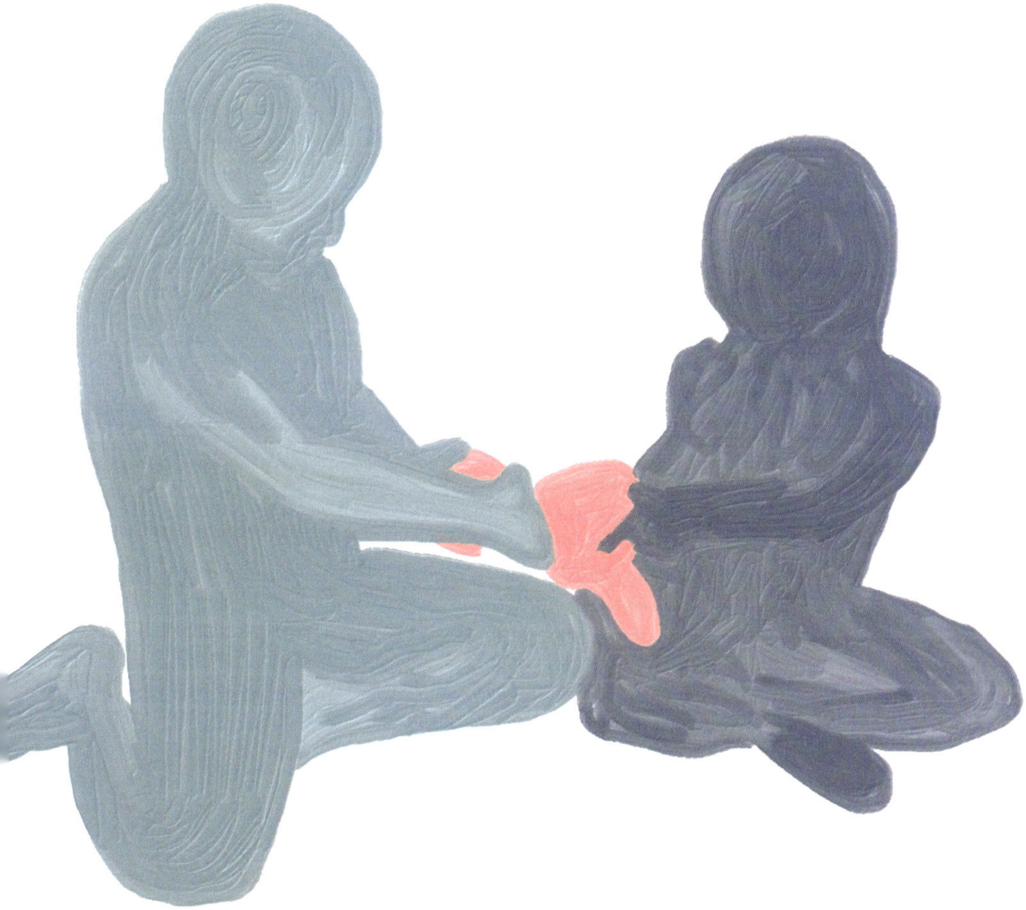

Sometimes, siblings need a break from each other.

Siblings learn things from spending time together,

things like being patient,
speaking up for themselves, and
putting others first.

Siblings can feel responsible
for each other.

Siblings don't want bad things
to happen,

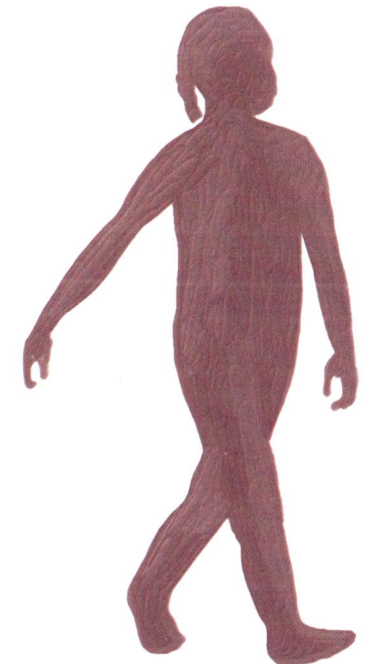

but, each sibling is their own person
who learns to make decisions
for themselves.

My sibling needs love and
attention from our family,

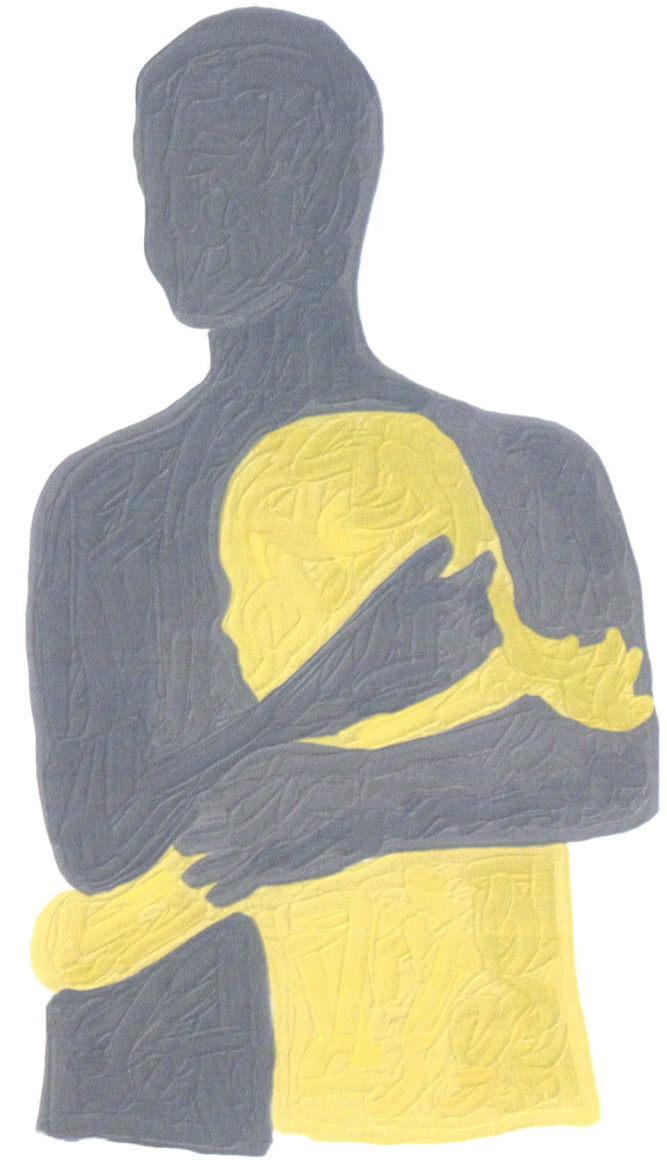

and , so do I!

Each sibling needs certain things to feel happy,
cared for, and challenged.

Those things aren't the same for every sibling.
Each sibling is different. Each sibling needs different things.

Since my sibling needs different things than me, it can feel like they get more attention than me.

I can try to remember that there is plenty of love and attention for all of us!

When I feel left out or jealous...

I can remember that there are times that I get to do things that my sibling doesn't get to do.

I can make a plan to do something with my parent sometime soon.

I can try to understand why it is important for my sibling to get attention.

Sometimes, I feel worried for my sibling.

I feel like I want to protect
my sibling. I wish the world
was nicer. I try to
remember that my sibling is
on their own journey, a
special journey no one can
take but them.

Sometimes, I wonder what life would be like if things were different. What if my sibling was older or younger or stronger or healthier or more like me?

A lot of the time, I love things exactly the way they are.

All of these feelings are okay.
I can talk about them, or I can keep them to myself.

Siblings have these feelings. I am not the only one.

I would not know all the things that I know,
think all the things I think,
or feel all of the things that I feel without my sibling.

No matter big or small,
no matter young or old,
no matter what is happening
in our family,
every sibling is important.

I am important,
and I can remind my sibling how important they are to me!

www.ingramcontent.com/pod-product-compliance
Lightning Source LLC
Chambersburg PA
CBRC090841120626
46551CB00008B/717